NATURAL PHENOMENA

NORTHERN LIGHTS

by Ben McClanahan

FOCUS
READERS

FOCUS READERS

WWW.FOCUSREADERS.COM

Focus Readers is distributed by North Star Editions:
sales@northstareditions.com | 888-417-0195

Produced for Focus Readers by Red Line Editorial.

Content Consultant: Dr. William Gutsch, Distinguished Professor of the College of Arts & Sciences, Saint Peter's University

Photographs ©: Stas Moroz/Shutterstock Images, cover, 1; V. Belov/Shutterstock Images, 4–5; Intrepix/Shutterstock Images, 7; Dr. William Gutsch, 8, 14, 16–17; Scott Kelly/JSC/NASA, 10–11; MSFC/NASA, 12; Paul Fearn/Alamy, 19; J. Nichols/ESA/NASA Goddard/GSFC/NASA, 21; SDO/Goddard/GSFC/NASA, 22–23; JSC/NASA, 25; Vadim Sadovski/Shutterstock Images, 27; GSFC/Solar Dynamics Observatory/JPL/NASA, 29

ISBN
978-1-63517-910-1 (hardcover)   11/19
978-1-64185-012-4 (paperback)
978-1-64185-214-2 (ebook pdf)
978-1-64185-113-8 (hosted ebook)

Library of Congress Control Number: 2018931715

Printed in the United States of America
Mankato, MN
April, 2019

ABOUT THE AUTHOR

Ben McClanahan is a writer who enjoys learning about science and nature. He hopes to one day see the northern lights in person.

TABLE OF CONTENTS

CHAPTER 1

LIGHTS IN THE SKY

It is a cold winter night. Stars shine in the clear sky. Suddenly, lights flash overhead. Greens, blues, and pinks appear high above the trees. Waves of color ripple and glow. This amazing display is the northern lights.

The northern lights are caused by charged particles that come from the sun.

The northern lights are also called the aurora borealis.

5

The sun constantly sends out streams of tiny particles into space. If these particles reach Earth, they collide with Earth's upper **atmosphere**. These collisions cause colorful lights to appear in the sky. The lights are called auroras. When auroras occur in the far north, they are known as the northern lights.

Each year, thousands of people travel north to see the lights. The best views are in places within the auroral ovals. Earth has two of these ovals. They are shaped like large doughnuts. One oval surrounds the north **magnetic pole**. The northern lights appear in this area. The other oval surrounds the south magnetic pole. The location of Earth's magnetic poles shifts slowly over time. Currently, the north magnetic pole is northwest of Greenland.

A TYPICAL AURORAL OVAL

Green auroras ripple across a clear sky in Norway.

In North America, parts of Canada and Alaska lie inside the auroral oval. In northern Europe, people flock to places such as Iceland, Norway, Sweden, and Finland. The northern lights can also be seen in many parts of northern Russia.

The northern lights can happen at any time of year. But they are best viewed during late fall and winter. At this time of year, the dark **polar** nights last many hours. The northern lights occur high in Earth's atmosphere. They form many miles above the clouds. For this reason, the northern lights are easier to see on very clear nights. Otherwise, clouds can block them from view.

SOUTHERN LIGHTS

Auroras can also form in the auroral oval around Earth's south magnetic pole. These lights are called the southern lights. They usually appear over remote areas, such as Antarctica and the Antarctic Ocean. As a result, fewer people see the southern lights. However, the southern lights sometimes appear over parts of Australia and New Zealand.

CHAPTER 2

COLORFUL COLLISIONS

Auroras happen because of charged particles from the sun. The particles move through space in a stream. It is known as the solar wind. To reach Earth, the solar wind travels approximately 93 million miles (150 million km). It can go as fast as 2 million miles per hour (3.2 million km/h).

Auroras appear when solar wind particles interact with the gases in Earth's upper atmosphere.

It takes two to five days for solar particles to reach Earth. However, the solar wind does not reach Earth's surface. Instead, the particles hit Earth's **magnetic field**. This field forms a protective bubble around the planet.

SOLAR WIND

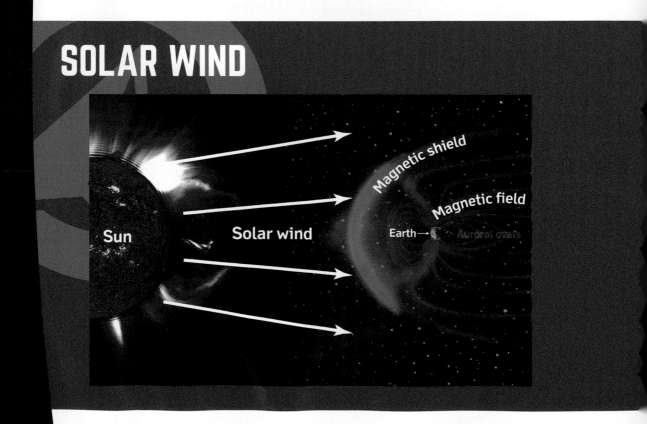

Sun

Solar wind

Magnetic shield

Magnetic field

Earth→

Auroral ovals

Earth's magnetic field steers the solar wind particles. It sends them toward Earth's two magnetic poles. This causes the auroral ovals to light up. The particles collide with the air high above Earth's surface. During these collisions, energy is released in the form of light.

Earth's atmosphere is made of several gases. Depending on which gases the particles hit, different colors can appear in the sky. Shades of green usually form when particles collide with oxygen. These colors tend to occur at **altitudes** of 60 to 100 miles (97 to 160 km). When particles collide with nitrogen, shades of red, orange, and blue appear.

The northern lights often appear as curtains of color.

These colors can form hundreds of miles above the ground.

Sometimes, high-speed particles from the sun come within 50 miles (80 km) of the ground. These particles can create purple or magenta colors at the bottom of an aurora. Some people have even seen splashes of pink.

The number of particles streaming down from space is always changing. The solar wind's effect on Earth's magnetic field changes, too. As a result, an aurora's brightness and shape can change often.

DANCING COLORS

Auroras come in many shapes. They can stretch across the sky in bands of light. Or they can be shaped like an arc. An aurora's lights often move. They might look like curtains flapping in a breeze. Sometimes many curtains of light spread out from one point in the sky. These curtains form what is called a corona.

CHAPTER 3

STUDYING THE SKY

People have watched the northern lights for thousands of years. Many cultures formed myths about them. In ancient China, for example, people imagined the lights were dragons fighting in the sky. The Inuit people of North America said the lights were caused by spirits playing a game in the sky.

In Finnish, the northern lights are called *revontulet*, which means "fox fires."

In Finland, people said a magical fox caused the lights. When the fox ran across the snow, its tail made sparks fly.

Legends about the northern lights still exist. For instance, some children in Norway are told it is bad luck to whistle at the northern lights. They are warned the lights will come down and carry them away if they do.

The northern lights have also fascinated scientists. For many years, people did not know what caused them. Kristian Birkeland solved this mystery. Birkeland was a scientist from Norway. He studied auroras in the late 1890s and early 1900s.

Kristian Birkeland (left) fired electricity at a metal ball in a vacuum tube to form a small aurora.

Birkeland thought solar particles and Earth's magnetic field caused the northern lights. To test this theory, he gathered a team of researchers. Together, they traveled to northern Norway. There, they recorded changes in Earth's magnetic field during auroras.

The data they collected supported Birkeland's theory. Birkeland even recreated the northern lights in his lab. He used a metal ball to represent Earth. Then he used electricity to imitate solar particles. A small aurora formed.

Other scientists did not accept Birkeland's theory at first. They did not

OTHER AURORAS

Earth is not the only planet that has auroras. In fact, they have been seen on almost every planet in our solar system. Only Mercury does not have them. Giant planets, such as Jupiter and Saturn, have large atmospheres. They also have strong magnetic fields. Auroras on these planets are often large and bright.

The Hubble Space Telescope has taken pictures of auroras near Jupiter's poles.

think solar particles could reach Earth. That changed in the 1960s and 1970s. **Satellites** studied Earth's magnetic field. They showed that the solar wind did affect Earth's magnetic field. Their images and measurements proved Birkeland was correct.

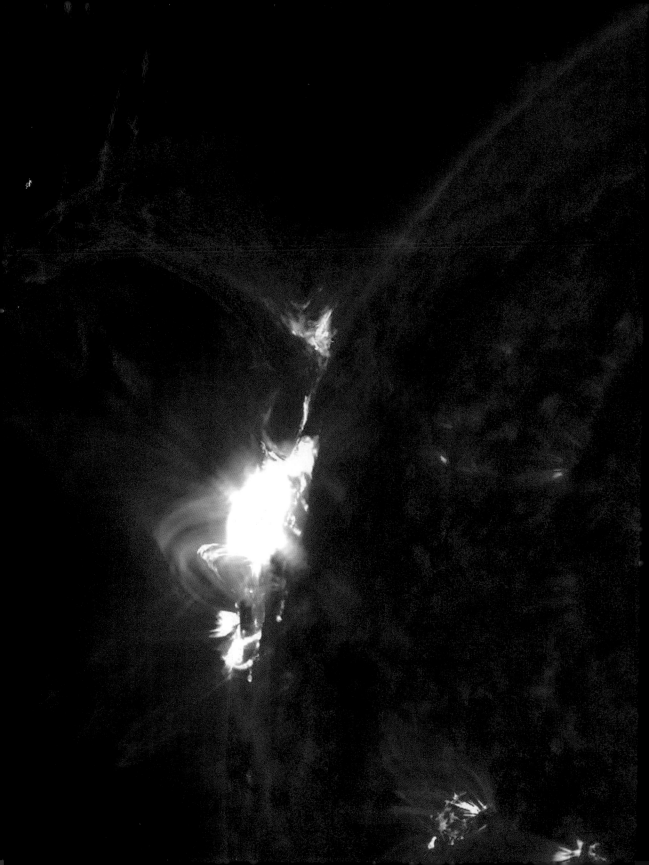

CHAPTER 4

SOLAR STORMS

Scientists have several ways to predict when auroras will happen. One warning sign occurs when large eruptions are seen on the sun. Some of these energy bursts are called flares. Others are called coronal mass ejections (CMEs). Flares and CMEs can increase the speed and **density** of the solar wind.

Flares and CMEs send huge amounts of energy out into space.

But those that do can cause geomagnetic storms. Scientists can track how much energy a solar storm releases. Solar storms can release massive amounts of energy. During a solar storm in 2012, Earth's atmosphere absorbed enough energy to power New York City for two years.

Satellites can help scientists track solar storms. In 1997, NASA launched the Advanced Composition Explorer (ACE) satellite into space. ACE recorded information about the solar wind. It also looked for solar storms. If one was coming toward Earth, ACE could send out a warning.

Satellites can help scientists observe auroras from space.

In 2017, ACE was replaced by a new satellite called DSCOVR. This satellite now watches for solar storms. Scientists also use computer models to predict solar storms. This technology helps people understand the northern lights better than ever before. But there is much more to learn about these amazing events.

ENERGY FROM THE SUN

Dark spots frequently appear on the sun's surface. These spots are known as sunspots. The number of sunspots varies. It follows an 11-year cycle, changing from fewer spots to more spots and then back to fewer spots again. When there are more sunspots, flares and CMEs are more likely to happen. These flares and CMEs can cause auroras.

Coronal holes can also lead to auroras. Coronal holes are places in the sun's atmosphere where the sun's magnetic field is weak. In these places, high-speed solar particles can stream out into space. Similar to flares and CMEs, particles from coronal holes can increase the solar wind's speed and density. When the particles reach Earth, they can cause auroras.

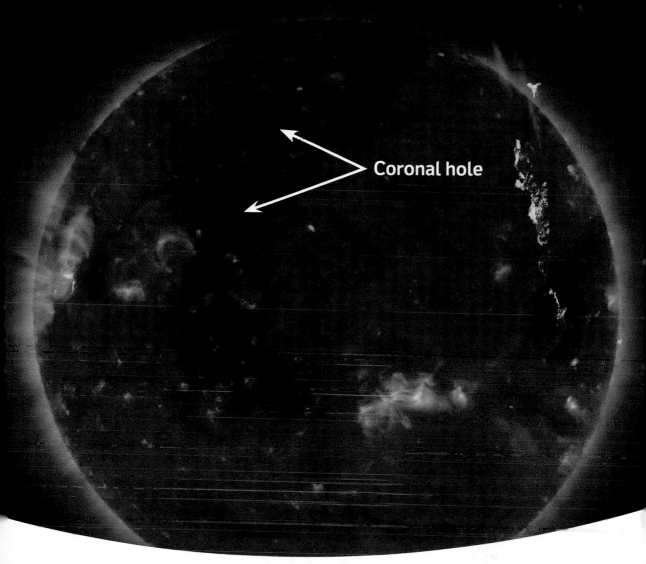

Coronal hole

Coronal holes look like dark areas on the sun.

Sometimes, there are more coronal holes when there are few sunspots. That means auroras can occur at almost any time, even when there are no flares or CMEs.

FOCUS ON
NORTHERN LIGHTS

Write your answers on a separate piece of paper.

1. Write a paragraph explaining what causes the northern lights.

2. Would you rather see the northern lights or the southern lights? Why?

3. Which color of light appears closest to the ground?
    - **A.** red
    - **B.** green
    - **C.** purple

4. Why are the northern lights harder to see on cloudy nights?
    - **A.** Clouds stop the solar wind from colliding with gases in Earth's atmosphere.
    - **B.** Clouds form above the northern lights and stop the solar wind from reaching Earth.
    - **C.** Clouds form below the northern lights and block a person's view.

Answer key on page 32.

GLOSSARY

altitudes
Heights above the ground.

atmosphere
The layers of gases that surround a planet or star.

density
A measure of how many particles are packed into a certain amount of space.

interfere
To mess up or get in the way of something.

magnetic field
The space around an object (such as a moon or planet) in which its magnetic force can be detected.

magnetic pole
One of the points where the magnetic field lines enter and leave a magnet or a planet.

polar
Near or in the part of Earth that is close to the North Pole or the South Pole.

satellites
Objects or vehicles that orbit a planet or moon, often to collect information.

TO LEARN MORE

BOOKS

Garbe, Suzanne. *The Science behind Wonders of the Sun: Sun Dogs, Lunar Eclipses, and Green Flash*. North Mankato, MN: Capstone Press, 2017.

Hudak, Heather C. *The Sun*. Minneapolis: Abdo Publishing, 2017.

Kenney, Karen Latchana. *The Science of Color: Investigating Light*. Minneapolis: Abdo Publishing, 2016.

NOTE TO EDUCATORS

Visit **www.focusreaders.com** to find lesson plans, activities, links, and other resources related to this title.

INDEX

Answer Key: 1. Answers will vary; 2. Answers will vary; 3. C; 4. C